An Hom

An Homage to Green Tea

Ch'oŭi

Translated by
Ian Haight and T'ae-yŏng Hŏ

WHITE PINE PRESS / BUFFALO, NEW YORK

White Pine Press
P.O. Box 236
Buffalo, NY 14201
www.whitepine.org

Translation Copyright © 2023 Ian Haight and T'ae-yŏng Hŏ

All rights reserved. This work, or portions thereof, may not be reproduced in any form without the written permission of the publisher.

Publication of this book was supported by public funds from the New York State Council on the Arts, with the support of Governor Kathy Hochul and the New York State Legislature, a State Agency and by a grant from LTI Korea.

Acknowledgements:
Excerpts of poetry, prose, and textual hybridity from *Homage to Green Tea* have been nominated for the Pushcart Prize and have appeared or are forthcoming in *Alice Says...*, *AzonaL*, *BlazeVOX*, *Blue Unicorn*, *Cider Press Review*, *Copihue*, *Kelp*, *Lalitamba*, *mercury firs*, *Moonpark Review*, *Paris LitUp*, *Plume*, *rivulet*, and *Runes*.

Thank you Beatrix Gates and Ann E. Michael for writing wisdom.

Illustrations: Elias Kuhlmann. Copyright ©2023 by Elias Kuhlman

Printed and bound in the United States of America.

ISBN 978-1-945680-71-7

Library of Congress Control Number: 2024930185

An Homage to Green Tea

Note: Romanization of Korean proper names follows the McCune-Reischauer system, as suggested by the Library of Congress.

Table of Contents

Introduction

Ch'ŏŭi was born with the family name of Chang in 1786 in Singi, a small Korean village. His father was a traveling peddler, and being something of a philanderer, was inattentive to family. When Ch'ŏŭi's mother and grandfather died near the turn of the century, he was orphaned, and so became a Buddhist initiate, eventually taking his Buddhist name, Ch'ŏŭi, meaning, "Simply Dressed."

At the age of fifteen, when Ch'ŏŭi first began his practice as a disciple of Buddhism, he resided at Unhŭng Temple. Unhŭng Temple, then renowned in Korea as an epicenter for green tea culture, is where Ch'ŏŭi was introduced to the ways of cultivating and drinking tea. These experiences would stay with Ch'ŏŭi for the duration of his life, helping to inspire "A Poem for Green Tea."

"A Poem for Green Tea" is a long poem originally written in *hanmun*, which is the Korean use of classical Chinese to write literature. The text of this poem includes short-short stories, legends, anecdotes, other related poems, excerpts from reference books on the subject of tea and green tea, and Ch'ŏŭi's notes to the poem. Taken as a whole, the poem seeks to authenticate the value of Korean green tea relative to Chinese green tea in a pleasing aesthetic manner, ending with an epilogue poem in praise of Ch'ŏŭi's green tea.

"The Divine Life of Tea" is more strictly prose,

but also centered thematically on Korean green tea. Ch'ŏŭi wrote on several occasions about Korean green tea. In his 1828 epilogue to the work, Ch'ŏŭi writes that his intention is simply to help a fellow monk with the task of writing an explanatory text on Korean green tea. He also tells of another purpose: to share an understanding of the harmoniousness of tea because it is not widely understood.

"The Divine Life of Tea" is a collection of instructions for how to arrive at the best cup of green tea. It begins with superb locations for the cultivation of green tea, when to pick the leaves, how to prepare and store leaves, ideal types of water, grades of boiling water, the utensils to use in preparation of a cup of green tea, and the type of company one should keep, among other topics. Ch'ŏŭi's prose in this section is not verbose but direct; one can learn about the particularities of the processes involved in creating an ideal cup of green tea, and the experience of drinking it. This section also includes notes from Ch'ŏŭi, but the notes are less extensive than those he made for "A Poem for Green Tea."

Knowledge of green tea and how to prepare it was limited in early nineteenth century Korea—even among noble classes. It was a chore to make fire. Few people knew the subtle qualities of water suitable for tea, or how to keep a luxury like green tea leaves; many people had never seen a green tea leaf. Both "A Poem for

Green Tea" and "The Divine Life of Tea" became and remain source texts for Korean green tea culture. This edited volume, *An Homage to Green Tea*, contains the full text of "A Poem for Green Tea" and an excerpt from "The Divine Life of Tea." The full text of "The Divine Life of Tea" and endnotes to that text are available for free download from the translator's website:

www.ianhaight.com/books

How to grow, roast, brew, and drink green tea are all part of the content, but *An Homage to Green Tea* is not merely a catalog of information; it is also a work of literature. "A Poem for Green Tea" is laden with clarifying commentary where Ch'oŭi thought such information appropriate. The commentary may contain anecdotal personal information, refer to a prior expert, quote a poem, or retell a relevant story. *An Homage to Green Tea* can be read as much for its literary context in a culture over five thousand years old as it can be read to learn about Korean green tea.

An Homage to Green Tea still has lessons for the contemporary reader. Chinese green tea was the source for misunderstanding the distinctiveness of Korean green tea during Ch'oŭi's lifetime. Ch'oŭi pinpointed the differences not only in quality and character of the leaves and tea, but also how differences in land, weather, and harvesting made the Korean green tea leaf unique in Asia.

Today, the uses of the Korean green tea leaf are

so numerous that in Korea, one can find candy, ice cream, noodles, toothpaste, deodorant, soap, and cosmetics—by no means a definitive list—made from the leaves. Within the past few years, the idea that green tea is a product good for one's health is common knowledge in some communities of the West, but the singular qualities of green tea grown in particular Asian nations remain largely unknown.

As longtime drinkers of green tea, we urge the reader to enjoy the exceptional pleasures of Korean green tea, pleasures that Ch'oŭi celebrates in *An Homage to Green Tea*.

—Ian Haight and T'ae-yŏng Hŏ

Translator's Note

Authored by a Korean monk, "A Poem for Green Tea" and "The Divine Life of Tea" were both written in *hanmun*, the Korean use of classical Chinese. *Hanmun* was the traditional language for writing literature used by scholars in 19th century Korea. Out of respect for the source text, *An Homage to Green Tea* is a translation of "A Poem for Green Tea" and "The Divine Life of Tea" from the original *hanmun*.

Hanmun is sometimes non-sequential in the flow of information. Words and ideas can appear haphazard and, to a Western reader, almost random. Although they are different texts, some of the information in both "A Poem for Green Tea" and "The Divine Life of Tea" is repetitive. *An Homage to Green Tea* is meant to provide a unified, sequential, and logical reading for the Western general reader. As part of the translation process, portions of "A Poem for Green Tea" and "The Divine Life of Tea" have been edited to render the most welcoming reading experience for this book's intended audience.

—Ian Haight

A Poem for Green Tea

The creator of mandarin orange trees
blessed another plant with virtues.

The creator
empowered the tea tree
to sprout deep roots
only in southern soils.

The tea tree's lush leaves
may freeze from snow
but evergreen, endure winter—
white flowers washed with frost
glisten in autumn
bountifully.

Tea blossom petals,
snowy-pure, white as the Immortal
of Guye Mountain—
the lustrous heart
of the pistil and stamens,
yellow as the golden light
of nirvana.

Midnight dew
washes clean
the jade-green twigs,
water from morning fog
condenses
on the narrowly-curved leaves,
the leaves, like sparrows' tongues.

The tea tree is like the luster leaf holly of China. Its leaves are similar to the gardenia, and blossoms to the briar rose—its core, golden-yellow. The tree flowers in autumn with a distinct, subtle scent.

Li Po once said, "Jade Well Temple in Jing County has pristine streams on every mountain and tea trees in abundance. Leaves and twigs like emerald-green jade—the Monk Zhengong always picks the leaves for his tea."

Heaven, Immortals, men, and ghosts
all love and respect tea—
I realize tea's nature
is a most brilliant mystery.
Shennong listed green tea
in his *Book of Food*;
since his enduring name
the tea has been compared to cream
and the sweet dew of heaven.

Always drinking tea gives man strength and a pleasant heart.

—from *The Book of Food* by Shennong

King Zishang visited the priest Luo Daijing. On Eight Proverbs Mountain, Luo shared tea with the King. After drinking the tea, King Zishang exclaimed, "This is heaven's sweet dew."

When you hear the sound
of wind in the pines
and rain on the leaves of trees,
remove the copper kettles
from the bamboo stove.
Wait until all becomes quiet—
a bowl of Spring Snow
is sweeter than cream.

—from Luo Daijing's poem,
"Boiling and Steaming"

Lord Zhou proved drinking tea
sobered those who were drunk,
and lessened the need for sleep—
Yan Ying of Qi ate brown rice
with tea leaves.
Yu Hong offered sacrifices,
begging Danqiuzi for tea—
Maoxian revealed thick tea shrubs to Qin Jing.

The wild walnut tree makes a bitter tea.

—from *Collected Definitions*

Picking the leaves from tea trees in Jing and Ba provinces and then drinking tea made from these leaves sobers one who is drunk from wine and makes people less drowsy.

—from *An Expansion of Definitions*

In *The History of Yanzi*, we find: "When Yan Ying was made Minister by Duke Jing of Qi, he ate boiled brown rice, three broiled skewers of meat, five eggs, and tea leaves."

The Book of Legends states,

Yu Hong from Yuyao went to the mountains to pick tea leaves; he met a priest pulling three blue oxen. The priest led Yu Hong to Waterfall Mountain, saying, "I am Danqiuzi. I've heard you are a connoisseur of tea, so I've always wanted to show you this mountain; it has a broadly-branched tea tree you can use.

Later, in the future, if you have tea to spare in your cup, I beg you to give it to me." Yu Hong kneeled and bowed to Danqiuzi, then entered the mountain's valley. He never wanted for tea.

Qin Jing from Xuancheng County picked tea leaves on Prosperous Power Mountain. He once met a person with hair over ten feet long. The person guided Qin Jing to the mountain's base, showed him a field of tea trees, and left. Later, he returned, took from his breast a mandarin orange, and gave it to Qin Jing. Overjoyed, Qin Jing then knew the tea was as precious as royal fruit. He departed, carrying his leaves on his back.

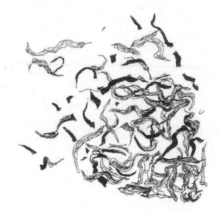

The dead buried in the earth
show gratefulness
for their families offering tea
by blessing them with wealth.

Tea is better
than the six accompaniments
for courtly banquets;
how the first Emperor cured his pains
is a mysterious story.

People once adored Startling Thunder—
Freshly Sprouted Purple
is now favorite.

The Book of Strange Tales states,

In Shan County, the wife of Chen Wu was widowed young with two sons. She liked to drink tea, and protected an ancient grave in her house. Before each drink, she repeatedly made offerings to the deceased. Her two sons said, "In his old grave, how can that useless dead man know your intentions? We'll dig up the man and take his body away," but Chen Wu's wife forbade it.

One night in her dream, the dead man said, "Though I have stayed here three-hundred years, your sons try to destroy my grave. Owing to your protection, I have enjoyed good tea. My bones decay in the sunken earth, but how can I forget that one good turn deserves another?"

In the middle of the garden at dawn, she found 100,000 coins.

Within the poem "Climbing to a Pavilion" by Zhang Mengyang, we find:

Kettles of royal dishes may be served,
and a hundred of them
praised for their exquisiteness,
but fragrant tea
is better than the six accompaniments—
its flavor overflows,
is prized throughout the nation.

In *The History of the Sui Dynasty*, we read,

When dreaming in his youth, the first Emperor of the Sui Dynasty's mind became afflicted by a god, an incident he continued to suffer from. One day he met a monk who said, "Tea leaves from the mountain can cure you." After the Emperor drank tea from the leaves, he was healed. Since then, the world began to know the importance of drinking tea.

In the T'ang record, *Enlightenment in a Forest Temple*, the Monk Zhichong produced three grades of tea. He wrote that guests should be treated to Startling Thunder, one should treat one's self to Day Lily, and that tea from Freshly Sprouted Purple was appropriate for services to the Buddha.

A T'ang court dinner
served 100 delicious dishes—
we only remember
Qinyuan's Purple Corolla Tea.
Since then, traditions
for early-picked tea leaves
have grown commonplace—
those who are pure, wise, and prominent
admire such tea's lingering flavor.

Emperor Dezong of the T'ang Dynasty often gave Princess Tongchang special dishes, including tea. Green Flower and Purple Corolla were the names.

The Book of Tea confirms that early-picked leaves have lingering flavor.

Decorating tea cakes
with gold-foil dragons
or phoenix
enhances the appearance,
but one hundred cakes
require 10,000 gold coins.

Who can fully realize
the genuine color and fragrance
of tea? A finger's touch
despoils a tea cake—
its true character
lost.

Large and small cakes of Dragon or Phoenix Tea began with Ding Wei, but were perfected by Cai Junmo. Both men mixed camphor with tea, and made a cake. The cakes, with dragon and phoenix patterns, were gilded, then offered to the royal court.

One hundred cakes
of golden-purple tea
cost ten-thousand coins.

—from a poem by Dongpo, untitled

In *The Complete Book of 10,000 Jewels*, we find: "Tea's original purity of fragrance, taste, and color is lost by one touch— the tea loses potency."

A virtuous monk
wanted to preserve his blessed tea
on a peak of Dream Mountain.
The monk grew five bags of tea
and made two blends
for the Emperor:
Auspicious Blessings of Gold
and The Saint of Willow Flowers.

Master Fu went to High Clear Peak on Dream Mountain, built a hermitage, and planted tea trees. After three years he harvested the finest teas, naming them The Saint of Willow Flowers and Auspicious Blessings of Gold. He gave five bags of each to the emperor.

The teas Snow Blossom and Ripened Cloud
compete in fragrance—
Two Springs and Infusion of Sun
have made Jiangxi and Zhejiang provinces famous.
The red mountain of Jianyang County
is well-known for clear water;
the quality of Moonlight on Mountain Streams
and House of the Clouds
is especially respected.

Rain on the Legs and Snow Blossom—
how these two are enough.

—from Dongpo's poem, "Response to Qian
Andao's 'Sending Jiangnan Tea'"

Shangu said, "I once picked high-mountain tea at my
house in Jiangnan."

Dongpo visited a temple where the Monk Fanying had
recently repaired a roof with care. As they drank fragrant
tea, Dongpo asked, "Is this a new tea?" Fanying said,
"This tea is a mixture of new and old, which makes the
scent and taste endure."

Zhejiang Province in China produces leaf tea, and the quality of Infusion of Sun is prized. Since the Jingyou Era, Two Springs and White Sprout teas from China have grown in popularity; lately, agricultural knowledge has increased, so the quality has improved. Their quality is much more than Infusion of Sun—hence, the tea leaves have become known as most precious.

In "A Casual Essay by Dunji," we read, "Tea from China's Jiangnan region is regarded by the world as best." It further states,

In the essay, "Sending Tea to the Minister of Justice" by Sun Qiao, we find these words: "I've sent fifteen packages of green tea with a lingering flavor to be offered at a shrine. The leaves were picked during The Season of Thunder, so be mindful of water for the tea's harmony."

Generally, the land of this tea—the red mountain in Ji-anyang County—has pure water. Moonlight on Mountain Streams and House of the Clouds are quality teas from that land; one should not use these teas carelessly.

In Master Tasan's poem to Zen Master A-am, "Asking for Tea," he writes:

In the morning, when flowers begin to open
and snowy-white clouds drift in the sunlit sky,
or when waking from sleep in the evening
and the luminous winter moon splits a jade stream—
these are auspicious times for tea.

Tea leaves grown in Korea
have the same character
as those from China—
the nature of the color,
smell, effects, and taste
is considered same.
The flavor of Luan tea is famous,
and Dream Mountain's
medicinal virtues are well known—
but above these two,
Tasan most highly prized Korean tea.

Within the *East Tea Record,* we find:

Occasionally the efficacy of Korean tea has been doubted—thought to be less than Chinese Yue teas. As I have observed Korean tea, the color, fragrance, effects, and taste have little difference from Chinese tea.

A Collection of Tea Fragrances says:

Luan tea has a famous flavor, and Dream Mountain has a strong medicinal nature, but Korean tea has both these qualities. If Li Zanhuang and Lu Yu were asked, naturally they would agree with my words.

To become young again
like a dried tree sprouting anew—
an eighty-year-old
will have a smooth face
like a heavenly red peach!—
one can attain
this miraculous effect.

I have a wellspring
and draw water pure as jade.
I boil the water in a stone kettle,
but sometimes I over-boil it—
how can I then bring this water
to a Seoul-city gentleman?

Li Po once said,

Master Chen of Jade Well Temple is eighty, but his complexion is like a peach or plum. The scent of his tea is untainted—different from others. Therefore, one can return to youth, like a once dried-out tree that suddenly sprouts leaves. People can live a long life with his green tea.

Yudang recently passed by Head Dharma Mountain in the south. After sleeping a night in my Purple Sprout Hermitage, he tasted the spring water, and then spoke: "The taste is better than buttermilk."

Su Yi of the T'ang Dynasty wrote "Sixteen Aspects of Boiling." The third aspect states:

Regarding over-boiled water: Water boiled to the tenth boiling is like men who live to one hundred. This water occurs occasionally because of inattentiveness; sometimes conversation is an obstacle; or sometimes the work is simply interrupted. This water should not be used for infusion because the water has already lost its nature.

Do you dare ask whether an old, pale, gray-haired man can draw a bow, shoot arrows, and hit his mark? Do you also dare ask whether this same man can climb a mountain with vigor, or make a long trip without fatigue?

The eighth aspect states:

Regarding Distinguished Jade Boiled Water: Stone is a condensation of the distinctive energies of sky and earth; its shape reflects this amalgamation. For the best kettle, carve a figure stone such that the character of the amalgam remains. How could water boiled in this stone kettle ever taste weak?

Nine difficulties must be overcome
and four fragrances preserved—
how can I teach you
who sit in meditation
on Floating Jade Hill?
To keep the four fragrances intact
one should not neglect
the nine difficulties.
If your leaves attain a genuine flavor,
they will be given
to the Palace of the King.

In the *Book of Tea*, we read:

Tea has nine difficulties: the first is making, second is discriminating, third is vessels, the fourth, fire, the fifth is water, sixth is roasting, seventh is grinding, eighth is infusing, and ninth is drinking.

Picking in cloudy weather and roasting at night should never be done. Tasting at the end of the tongue and smelling with the nose is not a method for discriminating. A burnt old kettle or smelly bowl are unsuitable vessels. Kitchen coal or gummy firewood do not make proper fires. Swiftly flowing water or still water are not good sources of water. A ripe outer leaf but raw inner leaf will not roast well. A dust-like green powder is not an appropriate tea powder.

Hands that hesitate or hasten will not brew a skillful infusion. Drinking too much in summer or too little in winter is not a healthy way to drink.

The Complete Book of 10,000 Jewels states,

These are the four scents of roasted tea: the first is authentic; second is like an orchid; third is clear; and fourth is pure.

If the inside of the tea leaf is roasted equally with the outside, then when brewed, the scent of the tea will be pure. If the leaf is neither raw nor over-roasted, the scent will be clear. If the roasting fire burns evenly, the tea will have the scent of orchids. Tea harvested before The Season of Rain for Grain has its essence preserved and an authentic scent.

In Blossoming Flower Valley on Chiri Mountain, tea trees grow widely over forty to fifty li. Tea fields in Korea are never wider than this.

Floating Jade Hill lies in a valley; at the base of that hill sits Seven Buddhas Temple. The men practicing meditation always pick their tea leaves late—sunrays dry the leaves to tinder brush. The tea, cooked like a boiled vegetable soup, is thick and a turbid red, coarse and bitter tasting. Thus, some monks have said: "The best tea in the world becomes deplorable through a clumsy hand."

When sweet green fragrant tea
enters the Court of the King,
brilliance extends in all directions
and every pathway opens.

Your divine roots
grow on the Mountain of True Wisdom—
an Immortal's jade bones
distinguish you
from all trees.

"Entering the Court" means "entering the heart."

Within *A Collection of Tea Fragrances*, we find, "For green foam that floats in the bowl, green powder should float in the air near the grinder." It further states:

Deep green tea has grown in distinction; its bluey-white foam is esteemed for beauty. Yellow, black, red, or pale foam mean the tea has no quality. Snowy-foamed tea is considered best, a bluish foam suggests an average tea, and a yellow-foamed tea is base.

A silk tent's shade
has an oddly favorable influence
on tea leaves,
so when heating
with a bamboo stove
in a tea contest,
the water must boil calmly.
When using a hot-burning pine charcoal,
choose pure water.

The tea, judged by richness:
the road fills
with fresh scents of tea—
people forget to return home.

—From Chen Meigong's
poem, "The Tea Contest"

When speaking of good tea
the leaves should be early-picked
with purple bamboo-like seedlings,
the roots in stony earth,
and leaves'
shaped like shoes of Huns,
oxen breasts, or patterns of waves.

Through a cloudless night
dew condenses on the leaves,
and the leaves, wet,
absorb it all.

Having skill in contemplation
increases
a praiseworthy tea's
fragrance.

In *The Book of Tea*, we read:

"Tea trees growing in a small gravel produce optimal leaves, and those in sandy soil are next in choice."

We also read,

"Tea trees that grow in a valley are supreme." The tea fields of Hwagaedong are in a valley and the trees grow in loose stones.

A priest came down from South Screen Mountain—
he came to infuse tea
with his contemplative skill.

—from Su Dongpo's poem,
"Seeing Off the Monk Qian"

Infusing tea leaves requires delicacy—
the secrets are difficult to describe.
Pure water and refined leaves
do not guarantee
the body and spirit of tea
will remain whole.

Though the body and spirit
may be kept intact,
be cautious
not to break
equilibrium—

one should not lose balance
for the co-existence
of sound body
and divine spirit.

A sip of Jade Flower
rises like wind—
the body lightens
as if walking high heavens.
The bright moon, a candle, and one's lone friend—
white clouds
form your surroundings.

Taste this Jade Flower Tea.

                    —from Chen Zhaijian's "Poem for Tea"

I only feel a freshening, lightly rising
chill of wind.

                         —from Lu Yuchuan's
                    "Poem for Seven Bowls of Tea"

Alone, solemn with a bamboo flute
and waves of pine
crisp cold freshens my body
enlivening my mind.

My guests: only a white cloud
and luminescent moon—

an enlightened priest
drinking tea
is most sublime.

Epilogue

The season's first tea from Ch'oǔi
steams scents of green,
the first bird-tongue leaves
harvested before the Season of Rain for Grain.
One need not mention
Moonlight on Mountain Streams
or House of the Clouds—
we smile at the year's full cup
of his Startling Thunder.

　　　　　—Written by Lay Devotee White Hill,
　　　　　　　　　Secretary to the King.

Excerpts from
"The Divine Life of Tea"

Well Water Does Not Make Good Tea

The Book of Tea describes mountain water as ideal, and river water as next best to use, while well water is inferior. If one cannot gather water from a river, or a nearby mountain has no spring water, the next best choice is to collect rainwater in The Season of Plum Blossoms. This water has a taste sweetly harmonious; since ages past, this water's nourishing quality has been well known.

Though snow water is clear, its nature is heavily dark, chilling spleens and stomachs of men. Unfortunately, this nature accumulates in the body if drunk too much.

Storing Water

To store water, the pot should be located under shade in a garden and covered with silk gauze. Let the water breathe the energy of early-morning's starlit dew. The benevolence will not disappear then; the radiance will always be preserved.

If the pot is covered with wood, stone, thin skins of bamboo sprouts, or is sealed by paper, and the pot is placed under sun, then the water's spirit will dissipate. The flow of energy will be blocked, and the water's spirit will be exhausted.

Only when tea is fresh and water divine is drinking tea a most precious thing. If tea leaves lose their freshness and water its divinity, what difference is there between tea from these components and ditchwater?

The Criterion for Boiling

There are three methods to observe boiling water, and each method has five distinctions to watch for. The first method is the criterion of bubbles, second is the criterion of sound, and third is the criterion of steam. "Bubbles" refers to the inner criterion, while "sound" refers to the outer criterion. Steam allows one to easily determine the aspects.

When bubbles are the size of shrimp eyes, then grow to the size of crab eyes, then fish eyes, and finally a connected beading, this is still an insipid state of boiling water. Continue until attaining a gushing boiling, like a rising wave's rolling shape, then remove the water from the heat. Wait until the surface of the water remains still. When all the water's energy has been transformed, it is then at optimum purity.

As the water heats, the first sound is that of a simple boiling. Next will be a rolling rhythm, like the turn of carriage wheels—then a shaking rhythm, like wind in bamboo trees. A sound similar to heavy rain will then follow, but these states of boiling water are still insipid. When there is no sound of boiling, the water is at optimum purity.

Steam may rise in threads of one, two, three, or four. If threads are disorderly, indistinct, chaotic, or tangled, the boiled water is still insipid. When steam rises in straight lines but separates into puffs, the water is at optimum purity.

The Harmonious Balance of Tea

When making tea leaves, the leaves should be refined.
When storing tea leaves, the leaves should be kept dry.
When infusing tea leaves, the process should be faultless.
Refinement, dryness, and faultlessness: these create a
complete harmonious balance of tea.

Epilogue

When it rained in the spring of 1828, I followed my master to Chiri Mountain. At The Temple of The Seven Buddhas, a copy of *The Complete Book of 10,000 Jewels* was brought down to me. I wanted to copy the "Record of Green Tea" section more concisely, but because of illness, could not finish.

When Suhong was my novice in the room for attendants, he wanted to know the harmonious balance of tea. He tried to copy the text, but because of illness could not finish. Hence, during rest from meditation, I wrote the book for him.

I ordered my brush to finish the writing. Once work has begun, it should be finished. Why should only Confucianists have such discipline?

My temple may possess knowledge of the traditions for drinking tea as a Buddhist practice, yet the Tao of tea is not widely understood. Therefore, I copied the text and share it with reverence.

— Mid-spring, 1830, written with care by Resting Hermitage,
ill, but practicing meditation, sitting near the stove,
the land outside, snow-covered

Endnotes

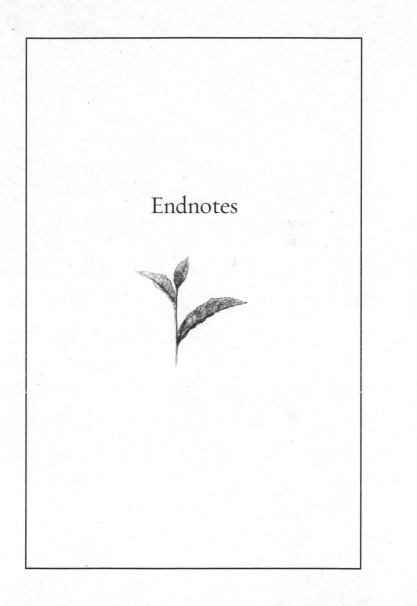

Page 19

Last two lines: The tea tree, typically cultivated to grow as a shrub, blossoms from October through December.

Page 20.

Stanza 1, line 3: Guye Mountain is the mountain home of an Immortal with skin like snow that drinks dew and rides clouds.

Line 5: Literally the *hanmun* characters translated here as "pistil and stamens" mean "kind-hearted" or "heart of beauty."

Lines 6-7: Nirvana literally is "Gold Rose River"—a river abundant with gold dust in India. As a metaphor, Gold Rose River represents nirvana in Buddhism.

Page 22

Line 8: Historically, cream was a drink of the privileged.

Line 9: "Sweet dew" is water from heaven said to make people immortal.

Page 25

Lines 4-5: Yan Ying of Qi's meal had brown rice as the main dish, while tea leaves were the side dish.

Commentary: Danqiuzi's leading three blue oxen is a device implying he is a Taoist Immortal.

The long-haired person (an Immortal) giving Qin Jing a mandarin implies the tea leaves were as good as the mandarin, then regarded as a divine fruit. Mandarin oranges were rare and precious in the Northern Chinese royal courts.

Page 30

Line 4: More literally this line could be translated, "by unsparingly rewarding with 100,000 coins those who offer tea." Traditionally tea was offered at a family altar for ancestors in the house.

Line 6: The "six accompaniments" are the six best things to eat or drink with food, including, for example, water and vinegar.

Line 11: "Freshly Sprouted Purple" literally is "the Purple

Fragrance of Deer Horn."

Commentary: Traditional Chinese houses were sometimes built over a tomb, encompassing it in the house's design. Due to a land's "feng shui," people wanted to build their homes in an auspicious location, even if a tomb was already present. Out of respect for the dead, the tombs were incorporated into the design of the house.

"One good turn deserves another" literally is "The hiding beneath a mulberry tree," which refers to an old Chinese story. In the Jin Dynasty, a high official named Zhao Dun was returning home from military training when he found a man, Ling Zhe, dying of starvation under a mulberry tree. Zhao Dun gave Ling Zhe some food, saving his life. Ling Zhe later became the bodyguard of the emperor. One day the emperor ordered Ling Zhe to kill Zhao Dun, but because Zhao Dun had saved Ling Zhe, Ling Zhe spared Zhao Dun.

The emperor's suffering could imply he suffered from headaches or tumors in the brain.

Literally the temple's name is "Enlightenment in a Forest," and the record is a record from that temple. Ch'oŭi's version differs from this original text, which states that

Startling Thunder was for one's self, Day Lily was for the Buddha, and Freshly Sprouted Purple was for guests. Startling Thunder was harvested first among all tea leaves, at least six days before the Season of Rain for Grain. The Season of Rain for Grain is sixth of twenty-four seasons on the Chinese agricultural calendar—about April 20 to 25. Day Lily was harvested third among all tea leaves, six to ten days after the Season of Rain for Grain. Freshly Sprouted Purple was harvested second among all tea leaves, one to five days before the Season of Rain for Grain.

Page 34

Line 4: "Qinyuan" was the name of the palace and garden of Princess Qinshui. That the only record of the dishes is Purple Corolla tea implies the tea was best among the dishes. The foam of the tea, also known as the "corolla" or "flower," was purple.

Line 5: "Traditions" refers to the traditional process for making tea from harvest, to roasting, to drinking.

Lines 6-7: The exact date of first-picked tea leaves is somewhat controversial due to differences in seasons and land between Korea and China.

Commentary: Purple-foamed tea is considered better than green-foamed tea.

Page 36

Lines 2-3: "Long" and "Feng" ("Dragon" and "Phoenix") are also the names of green tea blends.

Stanza 1: The teacakes were sometimes dusted with gold or wrapped in gold foil impressed with dragon and phoenix patterns, increasing their cost. Gold is considered to have medicinal qualities.

Page 38

Line 7: "Five bags of tea" more literally is "5 x 600 grams of tea," though the exact meaning varies due to differences in values of weight between China and Korea, and specific districts within the countries.

Lines 7-9: Master Fu began this tradition of growing tea for the emperor, which lasted over a thousand years. Such piety was a Confucian practice.

Line 10: "Blessings of Gold" in the name suggests the

core of the tea flower.

Page 39

Line 6: "Snow Blossom" is a powdered green tea with white foam on the surface and "Ripened Cloud" is a thick-leafed tea grown in high mountains. More literally, these two characters could be translated as, "thick leaves grown in clouds that surround mountains."

Line 8: "Two Springs" was a loose-leaf tea popular among scholars of the Northern Song Dynasty in China.

Line 12: "Quality" literally is "quality grades." Another more literal possibility for "Moonlight on Mountain Streams" is "Moonlight on Water between Cliffs," or "... between Mountains," all of which describe the landscape where the tea was grown. The majority of names given to green teas refer to landscapes where the tea was grown.

Commentary: The original Chinese characters for "Rain on the Legs" in Dongpo's poem mean "Two Legs." Ch'ŏŭi changed the characters; whether this was a mistake or according to his wit is unknown.

Fanying carefully repairing the roof implies drinking tea requires a well-attended environment. Fanying makes the statement about mixing tea because when an old tea is mixed with a new one, its characteristics are refreshed.

Ch'oŭi means to emphasize Zhejiang Province grows leaf teaf, as opposed to powdered tea. The Jingyou Era was during the reign of Emperor Renzong of the Northern Song Dynasty (1034-38).

The Season of Thunder is very early spring.

Page 45

Line 8: "Wellspring" more literally is "milk well," implying water from heaven, or like mother's milk. Water sprung from between stones that is soft, has no mineral taste, smell, or color is this kind of water.

Line 10: An ideal kettle should be made of silver.

Last line: "Seoul-city" literally is "South Mountain" in Seoul, a district for the very wealthy.

Commentary: "Purple Sprout" is the name of the best kind of tea leaf. Another name of the hermitage was "Bird on

One Twig" (Iljiam), inspired by a poem suggesting one twig was all a bird required to live on. The little hermitage was where Ch'oŭi lived.

"Water boiled to the tenth boiling" and "men who live to one-hundred" refer to the same quality of boiled water. Usually these idioms have a positive connotation, but in the case of tea and boiled water, it refers to the vitality of an old man at one hundred, implying a lack of freshness or potential because of long boiling.

Page 50

The inside of a leaf being neither raw nor over-roasted typically occurs from a thick kettle.

Page 51

"Forty to fifty li" is approximately four kilometers.

Page 52

Line 2: "Enters the Court of the King" more literally is "Tea presented to the heart," where heart refers to the court or king. Figuratively, this means to swallow.

Line 5: The tea tree's roots penetrate deep into the earth—even through solid rock—and can live for 1,000 years. This strength of the root allows tea trees to survive forest fires and remain green through winter.

Commentary: In Chen Meigong's poem, line seven, "calmly boiling water" is usually achieved by using oak charcoal.

Page 55

Lines 6-7: The rough stitching on the shoes makes it similar to a leaf's unevenness. "Oxen breasts" and "patterns of waves" are comparisons that also refer to the leaf texture. A leaf like the breast of a wild ox refers to the curvy protrusion of an Asian wild ox's breast. A curve like the shoes of a Hun could mean the top end of the leaf curls upward, or that the surface of the leaf has a coarse feeling.

Line 12: "Contemplation" could be translated as "samadhi."

Epilogue, Page 61

Lines 5-7: The implication is Ch'oŭi's tea is better than these.

Last two lines: Another possibility is "his Startling Thunder will give you a long life."

Appendix I:
Reference for Important Names

Note: Dates of birth and death are omitted here, if they are unknown in current historical records.

Cai Junmo: Cai Junmo (1012-67) wrote *A Record of Tea*, a book about green tea, on the orders of Emperor Renzong (1023-1063) of the Song Dynasty. Cai is also remembered for inventing "Small Dragon" and "Small Phoenix" tea cakes, which were made in a more elaborate process than ever before used. He was Chief of the Royal Tea Garden.

Chang Ŭi-sun: The initiate name of Ch'oŭi before he became a full-fledged monk.

Chen Jianji: The penname of Chen Yiyu (1090-1138), a minister and poet of the Northern Song Dynasty who was a member of the Jiangxi Poets.

Chen Meigong: Chen Meigong (1558-1639) was a calligrapher, painter, and tea specialist of the Ming Dynasty. He retired from his Confucian studies at the age of twenty-nine, and went on to write several books about tea.

Qin Jing: A well-known drinker of green tea. Qin lived during the West Jin Dynasty of Emperor Wu.

Chŏng Yak-yong: Master Tasan's ("Tea Mountain") real name was Chŏng, Yak-yong (1762-1836). A famous scholar at the age of nineteen, he was also a specialist in tea and mentor to Ch'oŭi.

Danqiuzi: A Taoist Immortal.

Dongpo: See Su, Dongpo below.

Dunji: Dunji or "Hidden House" is the pen name for Fan Zhengmin of the Song Dynasty. The essay is excerpted from a forty-six volume series entitled *Collected, Revised, and Expanded Criticism on Poetry,* Part II, Vol. 30.

Emperor Dezong: The second emperor of the T'ang Dynasty (58-76 AD).

"First Emperor": Emperor Wendi (581-604) of the Sui Dynasty.

King Liu An: King during the Han Dynasty (?-BC 122), Liu An invited eight immortals to his castle, but his guard found the men to all have white hair. Since the guard believed the men had no power to stop aging, the guard refused to let them meet the king. They then turned into eight boys and flew to heaven. One dropped a magic pill by accident, which was eaten by a hen; the hen also rose to heaven. Later, the immortals returned and brought the king to heaven. King Liu An was buried on Eight Proverbs Mountain.

Lay Devotee White Hill: The penname of Sin, Hŏn-ku (1823-?), a retired scholar at the time of the poem's writing.

Li Zanhuang: Li Zanhuang (787-849) was a minister of the T'ang Dynasty. He and his father were both high officials. Li served five emperors, but eventually was killed due to political intrigues.

Lord Zhou: The son of King Wen in the country of Zhou, brother of King Wu (1046-43 BCE) and Regent Uncle of King Cheng (1043-21 BCE). Lord Zhou helped King Wu by conquering the country of Zhou, and by acting as an advisor to King Cheng. Lord Zhou was a well-known politician who was respected by Confucius.

Lu Yuchuan: The penname of Lu Tong (795-835), Lu Yuchuan was a poet who in his day was as famous as Li Po. He never served at court but lived instead in nature, despite the emperor asking him repeatedly to serve at court.

Lu Yu: The author of *The Book of Tea*, the first book about green tea, which was a model for Ch'oŭi's "A Poem for Green Tea." Lu Yu lived during the T'ang Dynasty, approximately from 733-804. He became a respected monk after being taken in from the streets of Jiangling, where he lived as an orphan.

Mao Huanwen: At this writing, no information is available on the life of this person as mentioned in the text.

Maoxian: An Immortal covered with hair.

Master Chen: Master Chen was a famous tea drinker who had a strong vitality into his eighties.

Master Fu: Master Fu (497-569) was well versed in Buddhism, Taoism, and Confucianism. He built the hermitage in Sichuan Province, Northwest China, after returning from a trip to India. The mentioned seeds were obtained from there.

Master Tasan: See Chŏng, Yak-yong, above.

The Monk Qian: A monk respected and remembered as a Tea Master.

Monk Zhichong: A monk who lived during the T'ang Dynasty. Vagueness about his life and teachings has led to a number of interpretations as to how different teas should be used.

The Monk Zu: Zu created "drinking tea" Zen.

"Resting Hermitage": Another of Ch'oŭi's many pen names, which more closely translated reads, "Resting Hermitage, Ill, but Practicing Zen."

"Seoul-city Gentleman": Haekŏtoin (Hong, Hyŏn-ju, 1793-1864), a minister who asked Ch'oŭi to write "A Poem for Green Tea." Haekŏtoin was also the son-in-law of the king.

Shangu: The pen name of Huang Tingjian, a poet and calligrapher (1045-1105) who was a student of Dongpo. A provincial minister, Huang founded the West River (Jiangxi) poetry movement of the Song Dynasty.

Shennong: According to legends Shennong was a king of ancient China during the Longshan Period who tried all vegetables to determine their nourishing or medicinal effects. Shennong wrote *The Book of Food* based on his findings. Information on the tea tree first came from this book.

Su Dongpo: Su Dongpo (1036-1101), a poet who wrote a well-known long poem about leaving courtly duty and returning to nature. The name of the poem is "Replying to Jiang Kui's Gift of Tea." Serving at the emperor's court, Dongpo had many talents, including calligraphy and painting.

Suhong: Suhong was a minor attendant of Ch'oŭi's.

Sun Qiao: Sun Qiao, a famous writer and student of Han Yu (760-824) who lived during the T'ang Dynasty. Han Yu was the founder of "Old Style" poetry in China, and a high official of the Chinese court.

Su Yi: Who Su Yi was or when he lived and died is unknown.

Yan Ying of Qi: Sometimes known as "Yanzi," the "zi" being a title of respect. A man with the honorific "zi" in Chinese custom traditionally was to be remembered every generation after his death by his descendants, as opposed to four generations under ordinary circumstances. A virtuous minister known for his thrift, Yan Ying originated the belief that a thrifty man eats green tea leaves as a side dish. During the Zhou Dynasty (580?-500 B.C.) in China, Yan Ying served at court for thirty years. He earned the respect of Confucius, who considered Yan Ying a good model for a virtuous politician.

Yudang: Yudang (1766-1840) was the father of Kim, Chŏng-hŭi (1786-1856), one of the most talented calligraphers in Korean history. Kim, Chŏng-hŭi was a close friend of Ch'oŭi's; his influence is said to have contributed to the literary merits of "A Poem for Green Tea."

Yu Hong: It is unknown who Yu Hong was or when he lived and died.

Zhang Mengyang: A writer and high official who lived during the Western Jin Dynasty (265-316 A.D.).

Zheng Wei: Zheng Wei lived from 998-1063 in the Song Dynasty. He was the Chief of the Royal Tea Garden, and invented "Dragon" and "Phoenix" teas.

Appendix 2:
Lands and Locations

Dream Mountain: The five peaks of this mountain form the shape of a lotus, adding auspiciousness to the location. The number five is also significant to Buddhist, Taoist, and Confucian cosmologies.

Floating Jade Hill: A lower hill on Chiri Mountain in Korea.

Head Dharma Mountain: A mountain in Cholla Province, Korea—the southernmost, last mountain on the Korean peninsula. The earth energy of this mountain is said to be linked to Mount Paektu, the most sacred mountain to Koreans, and Mount Kunlun in China, the tallest and one of the most sacred in China. It is the mountain where Xiwangmu, the highest goddess in Taoism, is said to live. Yudang passed by Head Dharma Mountain on a trip home from exile.

Hwagaedong Dong: A place on Chiri Mountain.

Jiangnan: In Fujian Province, east of Jiangxi Province. A special tea for the emperor was cultivated there.

Luan: Luan is a province in China.

Mountain of True Wisdom: Chiri Mountain in Kyongsang Province. The literal Korean translation means a room reserved for the highest monk in a temple.

Shan County: Shan County is in Zhejiang Province.

South Screen Mountain: The mountain was named for the way it encircles the valley below.

Yue: An old country in the Chunqiu era of China (770-403 B.C.), near today's Zhejiang Province.

Yuyao: A county in Zhejiang Province, the historic land of the Yao family, which produced Emperor Xun, one of the most prominent figures in Taoism.

Appendix 3:
Ch'oŭi's References

The Book of Legends: By Dong Fangshuo of the Han Dynasty (154-90) who reputedly became an Immortal. As a minister, Dong served Emperor Wu (142-87), the second emperor of the Han Dynasty.

The Book of Strange Tales: Collected and edited by Liu Jingshu (390-470), an official of the royal court.

The Book of Tea: By Lu Yu, a monk who lived during the T'ang Dynasty; traditionally, *The Book of Tea* is the most important source text on green tea.

A Collection of Tea Fragrances: By Wang Xiangjiu, *A Collection of Tea Fragrances* was published in 1621, and begins with a section titled, "A Short Tea-list Preface." Who Wang Xiangjiu was, or when he was born and died is unknown.

The Complete Book of 10,000 Jewels: An encyclopedia with a special entry on tea by Mao Huanwen of the Ching Dynasty.

The East Tea Record: A book attributed to Chŏng Yak-yong, Ch'oŭi's teacher. Since the book has been lost to time, no one has been able to confirm this passage.

"How to Boil Water": A chapter in *The Complete Book of 10,000 Jewels*.

"The Nature of Wellsprings": A chapter in *The Complete Book of 10,000 Jewels.*

Sixteen Aspects of Boiling: Sixteen Aspects is a short book. The first three aspects concern how water is boiled, the next five discuss the kind of kettle appropriate to use, another five concern the wood to be used, and the last three discuss how to share the infused tea.

Bibliography

Chihŏ. *The Monk Chihŏ's Tea.* Seoul: Kimyŏngsa. 2003.

Ch'oe, Sŏng-min. *People Making Tea.* Seoul: Kimyŏngsa. 2004.

Chŏng, Dong-hyo and Chong-t'ae Kim. *The Science of Tea.* Seoul: Taegwangsŏrim. 2003.

Chŏng, Yŏn-sŏn. *A Poem for Green Tea.* Seoul: Nŏrŏkbawi. 1998.

Han, Sŭng-wŏn. *Ch'oŭi.* Seoul: Kimyŏngsa. 2004.

Kim, Myŏng-bae. *A Study on the Tao of Tea.* Seoul: Daegwangmunhwasa. 1996.

Korean Tea Poetry. Seoul: Daegwangmunhwasa. 1999.

The Chinese Tao of Tea. Seoul: Myŏngmundang. 2001.

Kim, Un-hak. *Korean Tea Culture.* Seoul: Irŭnachim. 2004.

Kim, Yŏng-mu. *Zen Master Ch'oŭi, Chang Ŭi-sun.* Seoul: Hanyŏngsa. 2004.

Lim, Hae-bong. *Zen Master Ch'oŭi and Tea Traditions at Taedun Temple*. Seoul: Yemunsŏwŏn. 2001.

Lu Yu. *The Book of Tea*. Yang-sŏk Pak, Trans. Seoul: Chayumungo. 1998.

Pak, Hŭi-chun. *A Cup of Tea*. Seoul: Sinu Lib. 1994.

Soam. *Green Tea Poem*. Seoul: Myŏngsang. 2001.

Tonggwang. *A Collection of Tea and Zen by Ch'oŭi*. Seoul: Pulgwang Press. 2003.

Yi, Tŏg-il. Chŏng, *Yak-yong and His Brothers*. Seoul: Kimyŏngsa. 2004.

Yu, Hŭng-chun. *A Critical Biography of Wandang*. Seoul: Hakkojae. 2002.

Yun, Pyŏng-sang. *Classsics on The Tao of Tea*. Seoul: Yonsei University Press. 2004.

Yun, Kyŏng-hyŏk. *Classics on Tea Culture*. Seoul: Hongikjae. 2004.

The Translators

Ian Haight's collection of poetry, *Celadon*, won Unicorn Press' First Book Prize. With T'ae-yong Hŏ, he is the co-translator of *Spring Mountain: Complete Poems of Nansŏrhŏn*, forthcoming from White Pine Press. Other awards include *Ninth Letter*'s Literary Award in Translation, and grants from the Daesan Foundation, the Korea Literary Translation Institute, and the Baroboin Buddhist Foundation. Poems, essays, interviews, reviews, microfiction and translations appear in *Barrow Street, Writer's Chronicle, Hyundai Buddhist News, Full Stop, MoonPark Review* and *Prairie Schooner*.

T'ae-yong Hŏ has been awarded translation grants from the Daesan Foundation and Korea Literature Translation Institute. With Ian Haight, he is the co-translator of *Borderland Roads: Selected Poems of Kyun Hŏ* and *Magnolia and Lotus: Selected Poems of Hyesim* —finalist for ALTA's Stryk Prize. Working from the original classical *hansi*, T'ae-yong's translations of Korean poetry have appeared in *Agni, New Orleans Review,* and *Atlanta Review*.

Companions for the Journey Series

Inspirational work by well-known writers in a small-book format
designed to be carried along on your journey through life.

Volume 14
White Crane
Love Songs of the Sixth Dali Lama
Translated by Geoffrey R. Waters
1-893996-82-4   86 pages

Volume 13
Haiku Master Buson
Translated by Edith Shiffert and Yuki Sawa
1-893996-81-6   256 pages

Volume 12
The Shape of Light
Prose Pieces by James Wright
1-893996-85-9.   96 pages

Volume 11
Simmering Away: Songs from the Kanginshu
Translated by Yasuhiko Moriguchi and David Jenkins
Illustrations by Michael Hofmann
1-893996-49-2   70 pages

Volume 10
Because of the Rain: Korean Zen Poems
Translated by Won-Chung Kim and Christopher Merrill
1-893996-44-1.   96 pages

Volume 9
Pilgrim of the Clouds
Poems and Essays from Ming Dynasty China
1-893996-39-5   192 pages
Translated by Jonathan Chaves

Volume 2
There Is No Road: Proverbs by Antonio Machado
Translated by Mary G. Berg and Dennis Maloney
1-893996-66-2   118 pages

Volume 1
Wild Ways: Zen Poems of Ikkyu
Translated by John Stevens
1-893996-65-4   152 pages